Robert A. Black

AMERICA,
WE HAVE
A PROBLEM

WHAT'S REALLY WRONG
WITH OUR GOVERNMENT,
AND WHAT *YOU* AND *I*
MUST DO ABOUT IT

ISBN: 147768820X
ISBN-13: 9781477688205

☆ ☆ ☆

TABLE OF CONTENTS

INTRODUCTION

On February 8, 2012, the Gallup polling organization reported:

A record-low 10% of Americans approve of the job Congress is doing, down from 13% in January and the previous low of 11%, recorded in December 2011. Eighty-six percent disapprove of Congress, tying the record high for disapproval set in December.

The report goes on to say:

Congress' current low ratings continue a generally negative trend. The 17% annual average for 2011 is by one percentage point the lowest yearly average Gallup has recorded. More broadly, the average congressional job approval rating since 1974 is 34%, signifying the generally poor esteem in which the American people have held Congress over the past decades. [1]

Clearly there is a problem with our government when 86% of us disapprove of the job Congress is doing.

I have written this book to answer two questions. First, what's really wrong with our government, and second, what *you and I* must do to correct the problem. My conclusions are based on an analysis of the political process from an outsider's perspective.

Today we are bombarded with messages from the Democrats and Republicans, the left and the right, liberals and conservatives, about what is right "for the American people." This book is unique because, even though it is about politics, it has neither a liberal nor a conservative bias. It is not about the virtues or vices of big government or small government or about fiscal largesse or austerity. It was not written to advocate the establishment of a particular policy or to promote the liberal or conservative agendas. The views expressed are not partisan, bi-partisan or non-partisan. In fact, they are unequivocally anti-partisan!

The messaging of the two parties is transient and changes whichever way the political winds blow. The message of this book is both timely, and timeless.

Like most of you, I have no vested interest in the political process except to vote and be subject to the legislation passed by Congress and signed into law by the President. However, also like most of you, I disapprove of the job Congress is doing.

A friend of mine, Raymond Farrar, said, "When you change the way you look at a thing, the thing you look at changes." My analysis of the political process has changed the way I look at that process. Consequently, the process has changed. Please join me in exploring why and how. And then, more importantly, join me in exploring what *you and I* must do about it.

It's important to know that I quote James Madison and George Washington in this book. However, I only quote them regarding their thoughts and experiences concerning the rise of parties, which they often referred to as factions. I also quote Glenn Beck, but only in regard to his thoughts on political arguments. I do not quote any of his punditry. I also quote the Virginia Declaration of Rights, June 12, 1776, and A Declaration of the Rights of the Inhabitants of the Commonwealth of Massachusetts, 1780. I only quote them concerning rotation in elective office.

I felt it necessary to include these caveats to ensure this book is not labeled a "conservative" work. It is not! It is critical to understand that because I do not want half the political spectrum to arbitrarily reject it simply because it might be labeled as such. Oh, by the way, that is a hint about one of the reasons why I changed the way I look at the political process.

CHAPTER ONE

AMERICA, WE HAVE A PROBLEM

"Insanity is doing the same thing over and over again, but expecting different results."

—Albert Einstein

Two days into their mission, the crew of Apollo 13 reported, "Houston, we have a problem." An oxygen tank had exploded in the command module, jeopardizing the astronauts' lives. One potentially fatal problem they faced was the buildup of dangerously high levels of carbon dioxide in the capsule. NASA's engineers immediately went to work to find a way to scrub the toxins out of the air knowing that the astronauts would die if they did not find a solution. What made their task even more challenging was that they had to engineer the solution using only materials that were readily available to the astronauts in the spacecraft. Because NASA had not planned for this contingency, the engineers had to think "outside the box." There was no guarantee of success, but they knew they had to do all they could to increase the astronauts' odds of survival. As we know from history, they were successful, and ultimately the astronauts did return to earth safely.

America, we have a problem! Our politics are toxic, infected by a contagion (Webster's: "corrupting influence")* that has led to a form of insanity. Please re-read Einstein's definition above. And, how is the insanity manifested?

Every election cycle candidates make promises to help themselves get elected. We believe them, and vote accordingly. However, the promises go unfulfilled and we get frustrated. During the next election cycle candidates again make promises to help themselves get elected. We believe them, and vote accordingly. However, the promises go unfulfilled and we get frustrated. During the next election cycle the same thing happens. And, during next the election cycle the same thing happens........... Each time we feel we do our duty by voting, but the people we elected aren't doing their duty. Why?!

The reason is our expectations and reality is very different. We expect those we elect (politicians) to do the difficult work of finding long term solutions for our Nation's problems. After all, that is why we elected them.

In reality, **once elected, a politician's first priority is winning their next election. Consequently, all their decisions, actions and messages (those things that constitute the politics they engage in) are carefully crafted to enhance their chances of winning that election. As a result the impera-**

---

* *All Webster's references used in this book were retrieved from http://www.merriam-webster.com/*

tive need to find long-term solutions for our Nation's problems is sacrificed on the altar of shortsightedness and the ambition to fulfill self-serving interests. Out of necessity politicians behave the way they do so they can extend their careers in "public service."

Here's one example taken from events leading up to the 2008 Presidential election. On January 31, 2008, CNN reported, "A Senate vote on an economic stimulus package must wait until next week, Senate Majority Leader Harry Reid said Thursday, allowing senators on the campaign trail to return to Washington." The Super Tuesday primaries were being held the next week on February 5th. Also delayed was a vote on a foreign intelligence bill. The report details Reid's reason for delaying the votes:

> The delay will allow Democratic Sens. Hillary Clinton and Barack Obama and Republican Sen. John McCain to participate in the votes, Reid said on the Senate floor. "I still have two Democratic senators [running for president]," Reid said. "As you know next Tuesday is Super Tuesday, and they're both very busy, as is Sen. McCain. So I probably can't get them back here until Monday, but I do need them back." [2]

Harry Reid specifically mentioned his fellow Democratic senators and stated they were "very busy." And what were they very busy doing? They were busy pursuing their own self-serving interests by running for President instead of doing the job they were elected to do and which we the taxpayers were paying them to do. Just to be clear, the Republican, John McCain, was doing the same thing. So I ask you, what do you think was the priority of those three career politicians? Whose interests were being served: the Nation's or theirs'?

It is important to note that Reid, who as the Senate Majority Leader, controls the scheduling of votes, delayed them to facilitate the self-serving interests of his three colleagues. He said he "must wait" until after the Super Tuesday primaries to schedule the votes as if some external force was compelling him to do so. Interestingly, the title of the article is, "Super Tuesday forces delay of stimulus vote."

On July 30, 2011, the Orlando Sentinel reprinted a truly timeless 1984 article by Charley Reese entitled, "545 people are responsible for the mess, but they unite in a common con." Reese provides several insights about why the Nation faces the problems it does:

 – Congress is the originator of all government problems and is also the only remedy available. That's why, of course, politicians go to such extraordinary lengths and employ world-class sophistry [Webster's: "subtly deceptive reasoning and argumentation"] to make you think they are not responsible. [Remember, Reid said the votes "must wait."]

- One hundred senators, 435 congressmen, one president, and nine Supreme Court justices – 545 human beings out of 238 million [300+ million today] – are directly, legally, morally and individually responsible for the domestic problems that plague this country.

- When you fully grasp the plain truth that 545 people exercise complete power over the federal government, then it must follow that what exists is what they want to exist."[3]

What does it say about our politics when "what exists is what they want to exist?" It says, America, we have a problem!

Clearly Congress (535 of those mentioned above) is infected with the contagion and merits our disdain. However, politicians are not the only stakeholders in the political process. How about us voters? Are we also infected? Do we contribute to the cycle of insanity? Is the two-party system a carrier of the infection? Don't the media and special interest groups feed the contagion as they seek to influence the political process?

The answer to all of the above questions is "yes." The reason is because no stakeholder operates independently in the political process: each relies upon the other as they play their interconnected roles. Because of that interconnectedness it is impossible to isolate a single source of the contagion that causes the insanity. Since the source cannot be isolated, it must be one that infects the entire political process. **The real source of the contagion is our current political culture.** Organizational behaviorists Don Hellriegel and John Slocum define culture as, "the dominant pattern of living, thinking, feeling, and believing that is developed and transmitted by people consciously or unconsciously, to subsequent generations." They explain:

> For a culture to exist it must:
> – be shared by the vast majority of a major group or entire society
> – be passed from generation to generation, and
> – shape perceptions, judgments, and feelings as well as subsequent decisions and behavior.[4]

Do dominant patterns of "living, thinking, feeling, and believing" dictate how the political process unfolds in our Nation? Does the vast majority of stakeholders in that process share those patterns? Does a political culture really exist? In chapters two, three and four I explain both explicitly and implicitly how our political culture has developed and how it operates to benefit career politicians to our Nation's detriment.

Hellriegel and Slocum explain that cultural values are the "collective beliefs, assumptions, and feelings about what things are good, normal, rational and valuable." Cultural values help shape individuals' "perceptions, judgments, and feelings" which subsequently affect their "decisions and behaviors."

So, here we are today and a large majority of us disapprove of the job Congress is doing. The question we must ask ourselves is, what does this situation say about what our current political culture values? Is this situation "good, normal, rational and valuable?"

America, we have a problem!

CHAPTER TWO

OUR POLITICAL CULTURE: THE HISTORICAL CONTEXT

Our political culture didn't just spring into existence. Its roots are intertwined with the history of our Nation. It has evolved over time and changed as the Nation changed. Our current political culture is very different from the one that existed in 1788 when the Constitution was ratified. This chapter provides the historical context in which our political culture evolved. The focus is on the ascendancy of the two-party system and the rise of political careerism.

From the Declaration of Independence we know that the United States was founded on the principles of "life, liberty and the pursuit of happiness." In our free society we enjoy the liberty to pursue our own interests. In pursuing those interests we tend to seek out and find others with the same interests. Political parties arise to pursue those interests collectively in the political arena.

James Madison, the "Father of the Constitution" and fourth President of the United States, wrote several of the <u>Federalist Papers</u> to support ratification of the new Constitution. In <u>Federalist No.10</u>, Madison wrote that the formation of parties is "sown in the nature of man." He stated, "...we see them every where brought into different degrees of activity, according to the different circumstances of civil society." He explained that parties exist because:

> A zeal for different opinions concerning religion, concerning Government and many other points, as well of speculation as of practice; an attachment to different leaders ambitiously contending for pre-eminence and power; or to persons of other descriptions whose fortunes have been interesting to the human passions, have in turn divided mankind into parties....[5]

The Constitution was ratified on June 21, 1788. George Washington was elected the Nation's first President. Following his second term he delivered his <u>Farewell Address to the Nation</u>. In his address he wrote about what he called "the spirit of party." Like Madison, Washington understood that parties would exist. As stated previously, Madison said the formation of parties is "sown in the nature of man." Washington echoed those words stating:

> This spirit...is inseparable from our nature having its roots in the strongest passions of the human

mind. It exists under different shapes in all governments....[6]

During his tenure Washington witnessed the emergence
of parties representing geographical interests. In his <u>Ad-
dress</u> he discussed the industrial North and agrarian South.
He provided a prophetic warning about the effects of the
"spirit of party" he was witnessing: "It agitates the Commu-
nity with ill-founded jealousies and false alarms; kindles
animosity of one part against another, foments occasionally
riot and insurrection."

Fast-forward approximately 60 years to the "insurrection" that erupted, the Civil War. Prior to the Civil War the
political battles over slavery were waged along a geographical partisan divide between the Northern Republicans and
the Southern Democrats. Democrats in the South chose to
secede from the Union rather than allow the Republicans
to impose their political will on them. At the end of the war
President Abraham Lincoln wanted to immediately restore
the union. However, there was a faction within the Republican Party, called the Radicals, which wanted to retaliate
against the South.

Lincoln's assassination ensured that reconciliation
would not occur and left the Radicals virtually unchecked
in their retaliatory actions. As a result the animosity of the
Southern Democrats deepened under the onslaught of the
Radicals and their political dominance. Adding insult to
injury the Radicals passed the harsh Reconstruction Acts

to punish the South. Southern Democrats were unable to assent to the laws and had no recourse but to acquiesce to the will of the Radical Republicans.

In his <u>Address</u> George Washington warned that a "spirit of revenge" is "natural to party dissention" and that it resulted from the "domination of one faction [party] over another." The domination of the Republicans over the Democrats prior to and following the Civil War, led to party dissension and provoked a "spirit of revenge."

As the Nation grew during the 19th century the political power of the Democratic Party and Republican Party increased. A "two-party system" emerged in which the two major parties began to dominate the entire political landscape of the United States. There were third parties in the late 19th and early 20th centuries, but none ever really challenged the supremacy of the Democrats and the Republicans for political power.

Also, during the 20th century political careerism became the norm and assumed a prominent role in our political culture. How did this come about?

On February 3, 1913, the 16th Amendment, the income tax, was ratified. With the power to collect more revenue, Congress began to spend more. Once voters realized they could enrich themselves with benefits through the legislative process, a symbiotic relationship developed between themselves and their elected representatives.

As voters developed an appetite for government benefits, politicians developed spending habits to satisfy that appetite. It's kind of like the old conundrum, "Which came first, the chicken or the egg?" Did voter demand come first, or did politicians' spending come first? Either way, voters wanted what politicians could give – benefits, and politicians wanted what voters could give – electoral victories.

As Congress increased its role as the benefactor of society, the political process became increasingly complex. The importance of politics, and subsequently, the power of politicians, increased correspondingly. Inevitably, competition for political action ensued as the interests of one group came into conflict with the interests of other groups. Consequently, voters became more beholden to politicians as they sought to protect their piece of the benefits pie. Eventually, a governing class emerged, and seeking long careers in "public service" became the norm.

CHAPTER THREE

OUR POLITICAL CULTURE AND MAINTAINING THE POLITICAL STATUS QUO
PART ONE

"The culture you live with sustains the system you live under."

—Raymond Farrar

Nearly all of us disapprove of the job Congress is doing. We are frustrated, but nothing really changes. The reason – the political status quo is maintained. The pivotal feature of our current political culture is the battle for party dominance between the Democratic Party and the Republican Party. The outcome of that battle determines which party will be in the majority and which party will be in the minority. Being the majority party means being the party in power. The leaders of the majority party hold the positions of power. Politicians want power! Each biennial election cycle the potential exists for the balance of power to shift from one party to the other.

In part one of this chapter I discuss the means used by the two-party system to maintain the political status quo. In PART TWO I focus on the role voters play.

Article 1, Section 5, of the Constitution states, "Each House may determine the Rules of its Proceedings." The two parties use this provision of the Constitution to help maintain the political status quo. They have adopted rules in both the House of Representatives and the Senate that empower the majority party.

As stated previously, after completion of each biennial election cycle, one party is in the majority and one party is in the minority in one or both houses of Congress. During the current 113th Congress, Republicans are the majority in the House and Democrats are the majority in the Senate. At the start of each Congress (a Congress sits for two years and consists of two sessions) the parties pick their respective members to serve on committees. Since one party always has more members, that party gets a greater number of seats on each committee. Independents are required to declare which of the two parties they will align with so the majority/minority standing can be determined. Once the committee assignments are made the members elect the committee chairman. Because the majority party has the most members on the committee, the chairman is invariably selected from that party. Usually, the most senior member of the majority party is selected chairman.

In addition to using the very mechanisms of government to maintain the political status quo, the parties use other subtle, yet very powerful means, to influence stakeholder behaviors. Employing those means facilitates their battles for dominance.

Party identification is one means employed by the two parties. The Democrats and the Republicans have a virtual monopoly on party identification. Candidates must align themselves with either the Democratic Party brand or the Republican Party brand if they expect to have any real chance of getting elected. The brand is so important, that a D or an R follows politicians' names to distinguish their party affiliation.

Controlling the language of the political argument is another means. Entertainer and political commentator Glenn Beck said, "Control the language to control the argument."[7] He made the comment in the context of political correctness, but it can be applied in the much broader context of politics. The leadership of the two parties controls the language of all political arguments and shapes those arguments to support their partisan political objectives.

According to current political dogma the Democratic Party is the guardian of liberal ideology and controls the language of liberalism. The Republican Party is guardian of the conservative ideology and controls the language of conservatism. The parties jealously guard the ownership of their respective sides of the argument. If your principles and interests don't fit neatly into one of those boxes, you're kind of stuck. This aspect of maintaining the political status quo is evidenced by the rise and subsequent marginalization of the Tea Party movement by the Republican Party.

Tea Party leaders claimed theirs was a grassroots movement that advocated smaller government, less government intrusion, etc. The Tea Party garnered a lot of media attention and provided fodder for bloggers and political pundits. The prevailing language of the liberal vs. conservative argument ensured their positions were labeled "conservative," hence Republican – Republican because the Republican Party controls the language of conservatism.

For a while the Republican Party leadership wasn't quite sure how to deal with the Tea Party upstarts. They had to carefully craft their messaging not to alienate the Tea Partiers. After all, since Tea Partiers are conservatives, the party needed their votes to win elections. At the same time they had to distance themselves from the more radical elements of the movement, which threatened the party's ability to win elections. Ultimately, the Republican Party leadership knew they only had to wait for the media attention to subside and then the political status quo would return.

The artful use of language by politicians allows them to convey the message that they are working for "the American people," when in actuality they are working on self-serving and partisan interests. Politicians use language to engage in the art of sophistry. Webster's defines sophistry as, "subtly deceptive reasoning or argumentation." Wikipedia, the online encyclopedia, states:

In modern usage, *sophism, sophist* and *sophistry* are derogatory terms. A *sophism* is taken as a specious argument used for deception. It might be crafted to appear logical while actually representing a falsehood, or it might use obscure words and complicated sentence constructions in order to intimidate the opponent into agreement out of fear of feeling foolish. Other techniques include manipulating the opponents' prejudices and emotions to overcome their logical facilities.[8]

During the debate over health care reform, Obama changed the language of the argument to health insurance reform. Why did he do that? Did the legislation change because of the name change? Of course it didn't. By changing the name to health insurance reform, Obama put a face on the problem, the greedy insurance companies, appealing to our emotion and prejudices. Consequently, we burned up the blogs. While we were busily distracted, the two parties resumed their slugfest over health care reform with each side looking to gain some political advantage.

How often do we hear the parties' leadership claiming "the American people" want this or that? For example, the leaders invariably invoke the will of "the American people" with regards to bipartisanship. Each party claims it is attempting to work in a bipartisan manner while the other party is engaging in partisan politics for political gain. Their messaging is designed to build the perception that their party is working on behalf of "the American people" while the other party is being obstructionists. If you examine this type of argument closely, you will begin to realize that it is an example of sophism. It seems logical, but it is really designed to deceive and divide us.

On September 5, 2011, the Associated Press carried a report entitled, "Obama says GOP must back US first, create jobs." President Obama was in Detroit, Michigan, for a Labor Day rally. In the article Obama is quoted as saying, "I believe both parties can work together [bipartisanship] to solve our problems."[9] Here he is trying to sound presidential and above the political fray. However, being a politician, he could not pass up the opportunity to take a swipe at the opposition: "We're going to see if we've got some straight shooters in Congress. We're going to see if congressional Republicans will put country before party." The implication, Republicans are only interested in engaging in partisan politics for political gain.

The proliferation of partisan polling, and the reporting of polling data, constitutes another form of sophism used by the political parties and the party leadership to support their personal and partisan political ambitions. Their goal is to manipulate our behavior by building perceptions that they effectively manufacture. Please see "Polling, Messaging and Perception" at the end of this part of Chapter Three for additional comments on polls and polling.

Politically it is tougher for the majority party (the party in power) because they have to craft their strategy and messaging to ensure "the American people" know all the good they are doing on their behalf. For the minority party, crafting their political strategy and messaging is easier. They only need to point out how the majority party's policies are failing "the American people."

The media is complicit with the leadership of the two parties in their efforts to maintain the political status quo. The media carries the party message to the public. Media outlets have either a liberal or conservative bias in their reporting and analysis, and their bias is not subtle. The media reports on what politicians do and say, focusing primarily on the party leadership. The media has to fill up the 24-hour news cycle so they cover politics in great detail. Political pundits provide their expert commentary about what politicians say and spin their commentary to influence our thinking; their bias is also not subtle.

Perhaps the most important facilitator is m-o-n-e-y, money! The two parties raise and spend the preponderance of money during campaigns. The Democratic National Committee (DNC) and its Republican counterpart (RNC), the Democratic Congressional Campaign Committee (DCCC) and its Republican counterpart (RCCC), the Democratic Senatorial Campaign Committee (DSCC) and its Republican counterpart (RSCC) are prolific fund raising operations. They funnel the money they raise to campaigns of candidates they feel are the most "electable."

Couple the parties' fund raising prowess with the money raised and spent by Political Action Committees (PAC) and Super PACs, which include big moneyed special interests, and the amount spent on campaigns can reach hundreds of millions of dollars every election cycle. Throw in a

Presidential election and the amount spent can reach a billion dollars.

How does the ability to raise and spend large amounts of money on campaigns help maintain the political status quo? The parties and their media allies build the perception in voters' minds that a candidate is only viable, and thus electable, if he is able to raise and spend large amounts of money to support his campaign. Candidates generally must rely on their party and special interest benefactors to raise enough money to compete unless they happen to be independently wealthy. Even then, most don't spend their own funds and look to the parties for support. The result is that Democratic candidates and Republican candidates are the only ones that can raise the large sums of cash to be considered viable. Consequently, only Democrats and Republicans are perceived as electable.

At this point Charley Reese's comment is worth repeating, "When you fully grasp the plain truth that 545 people exercise complete authority over the federal government, then it must follow that what exists is what they want to exist." The parties use identification, language, the media and money as the means to ensure stakeholders engage in behaviors that are reasonably predictable and which support maintaining the political status quo. It is important that voters continue to vote the way they always have and that the media continues exploiting the sensational and reports in accordance with their bias. It is also important that big moneyed interests continue their attempt to buy access and exert influence on the political process. Essentially, all stakeholders in the political process must behave in accordance with expectations.

Why is maintaining the political status quo so important? The answer lies in who benefits the most. Career politicians benefit the most because maintaining the political status quo provides a framework in which they can pursue their own self-serving and self-aggrandizing interests.

Polling, Messaging and Perception

Who loves polls? Pollsters love polls! Politicians love polls! The media loves polls! And why – pollsters make money, politicians adjust their messaging and the media has something to report. But, what do polls really tell us? With partisan polling that's easy. Partisan polling is designed to build a perception in our minds that "the American people" support a particular policy or that "the American people" are opposed to a certain policy, or that one party is "winning" over "the American people" in their campaigns. Those polls are designed to manipulate voters.

Prior to the 2010 election cycle POLITICO.com reported, "Dems push with torrent of polls." The author explained that the Democrats engaged in partisan polling to counter the Republican Party's momentum in building the perception that they would take control of the House from the Democrats. The article spells out what the Democrats were attempting to do:

Democratic lawmakers and House candidates have released a flood of internal polling data in recent days, aimed at countering the perception that Republicans have the majority within their grasp and numerous Democratic-held seats are as good as gone. Some of the Democratic polls have shown highly vulnerable districts still winnable for the party. The big-picture case the party is making – to an audience that includes members, donors and voters – is that Democrats are in a solid position to defend their hold on Congress, with a wall of well-positioned incumbents poised to turn back a Republican electoral tide.

The report clarifies that:

The data dump comes after allowing months of Republican polling to go unanswered and just weeks after multiple national polls – from ABC News and the Washington Post and from NBC and the Wall Street Journal – gave Republicans a strong lead on the generic ballot, and several top political handicappers predicted that Republicans would take control of the House. [10]

What about polls conducted by so-called "non-partisan" public polling organizations such as Quinnipiac University? Campaigns release polling data and organizations like

Quinnipiac release polling data, but which is accurate and which should be trusted?

In 2010 POLITICO.com carried another report on polling entitled, "Polls become another spin weapon." In this article the author states, "Forget the careful craft of survey research; as the midterm election hurtles toward the finish, campaigns are wielding polls less like scientific instruments than like heavy weaponry, using them to hijack news cycles and push their favored narratives about the campaign." He says it is a "shrewd way to exploit one of the media's tough election-year quandaries," which polls to trust. He goes on to explain:

> All that uncertainty means that day to day campaigns can pretty much choose whatever version of the facts they want, blasting out public and internal polling data – even when the numbers aren't exactly ironclad. While strategists privately study data to make calls about television ads and campaign travel, they selectively leak data and hype or knock down public surveys almost entirely in the service of driving media coverage, courting donors and firing up volunteers.

The author quotes Ken Spain, Communications Director for the National Republican Congressional Committee, "Positive poll numbers translate into momentum and money for a campaign."

What is the tactic?

> The Florida governor's race was the setting of one high-profile polling duel...Quinnipiac University released a survey showing Republican health care executive Rick Scott leading Sink [the Democratic candidate] by 6 percentage points, 49 to 43 percent. Sink's campaign responded by releasing some of its own polling: a survey from the Democratic firm Hamilton Campaigns that had Sink 1 point ahead of Scott, 45 percent to 44 percent.

The above example addresses how a Democratic candidate employed the tactic. The author also provides an example of how a Republican candidate employed the tactic, highlighting the fact that both parties engage in the same practice:

> The same approach works for both parties: When the Democratic Senatorial Campaign leaked an internal poll in mid-September showing Louisiana Rep. Charlie Melancon within 10 points of unseating Republican Sen. David Vitter, the GOP firm Magellan Strategies put out a survey the same day that had Vitter ahead, 52 percent to 34 percent, in an attempt to extinguish any potential story line that suggested the race was tightening. [11]

Earlier in this chapter I provided the Webster's dictionary definition for sophism: "subtly deceptive reasoning or argumentation." The parties are engaging in sophistry by attempting to mislead us with their polling. The bottom line is we must not let polls make up our minds about issues or candidates – that is really just a cop-out and exactly what the parties want. Instead we must think for ourselves and make informed decisions.

PART TWO

In this part of the chapter I focus on voters and how their behaviors help to maintain the political status quo. If we wonder why Congress is so dysfunctional, we must look in the mirror. After all, we do still hold elections.

Frederic Bastiat was a political commentator in France. He wrote a book called The Law, in which he offers insights about how legislators view voters:

How does he regard the people when a legislator is to be chosen? Ah, then it is claimed that the people have an instinctive wisdom; they are gifted with the finest perception; *their will is always right; the general will cannot err....* His will and capacity to choose wisely are taken for granted. Can the people be mistaken? Are they not adults? Are they not capable of judging for themselves? Do they not know what is best for themselves? They desire to manage their own affairs, and they shall do so."

However, Bastiat goes on to explain, that once elected the legislator's view of voters change:

> But, when the legislator is finally elected – ah! Then indeed does the tone of his speech undergo a radical change. The people are returned to passiveness, inertness, and unconsciousness; the legislator enters into omnipotence. Now it is for him to initiate, to direct, to propel and to organize. Mankind only has to submit....[12]

The Law was first published in 1850. However, that principle still holds true in 2012.

Today what our elected officials do is even more insidious. They build the perception in our minds that we play a meaningful role in the political process. Sociologist Jacques Ellul wrote a book, Propaganda: The Formation of Men's Attitudes, in which he spells out how this is accomplished:

> ...governmental propaganda suggests that public opinion demands this or that decision; it provokes the will of the people, who spontaneously would say nothing. But, once evoked, formed, and crystallized on a point, that *will* becomes the *people's will*; and whereas government really acts on its own, it gives

the impression of obeying public opinion – after first having built that public opinion. The point is make the masses demand of the government what the government has already decided to do.[13]

The last statement is especially telling.

In the political process we are mere sheep to be shepherded by our political masters. However, in this case the setting is not pastoral and the shepherds are not benevolent. They exploit the sheep for their own gain. They like passive sheep, because passive sheep are easier to corral and thus control. As Bastiat emphasized, we need but "submit" to their will.

As I explained in Chapter One, as voters we must wake up to the fact that our expectations do not measure up to reality. Picture yourself in the voting booth. You are standing there to cast your vote. You review the list of candidates, trying to remember all the promises the candidates made during their campaigns. You cast your vote. There, you're done. You have done your civic duty. You leave the polling place with the hope your candidate wins and will go to Washington and work hard to fulfill the campaign promises he made. That is your expectation; reality is something completely different.

All the promises your chosen candidate made to secure your vote are really pretty much bogus. In Washington he only has one vote in the legislative process. There are 535 others in the House, Senate and White House that have a say about which legislation becomes law. There are nine others, the Justices of the Supreme Court, who also have a say if the legislation is subjected to judicial review.

The biggest divergence between your expectations and reality occurs when your guy gets to Washington. You helped elect him and expect him to go to work for you. You expect him to represent your interests and to work with his fellow Congressmen and women to find long-term solutions to our Nation's problems. However, once he arrives he immediately begins to work on his re-election bid.

On August 12, 2011, Yahoo carried a blog entry on its "The Ticket" page by Rachel Rose Hartman entitled, "Poll suggests 2012 change in power in Washington." In the entry Ms. Hartman sites a USA Today/Gallup poll: "Only 24 percent of all adults surveyed in the poll said most members of Congress deserve re-election 'the lowest percentage since Gallup began asking the question in 1991.'" The entry also states, "However, the poll shows that 56 percent of adults believe their own representative deserves re-election."[14]

Again, more evidence that we disapprove of the job Congress is doing. However, something doesn't add up. 76% of those polled either didn't care, or thought that most members of Congress do not deserve re-election, a fairly substantial majority. But, a majority from the same polling population, albeit smaller, also thinks their own representative deserves re-election. The attitude seems to be, your guy is the problem, not mine. You vote your guy out because I'm going to keep voting for my guy.

Who has the courage to follow their convictions and vote their own guy out; apparently not enough people to make any real difference. Consequently, we continue to help maintain the political status quo, which serves the interests of career politicians to our own detriment.

I talked to a gentleman at a political rally a couple of years ago. I asked him if he would vote for an independent or third party candidate. He said he would, if he thought the candidate could win. We have allowed the parties to scare us into not taking responsibility for our own vote. The parties have perpetrated a sophism that helps ensure only a Democrat or a Republican will be elected.

If an independent or third party candidate enters a race he is labeled either a liberal or a conservative. Remember, the parties own that language and use it to maintain the political status quo for their own benefit. Once that labeling occurs, the party, whose ideology the candidate is likened to, immediately begins the process of scaring voters, virtually ensuring the candidate has no chance of being elected. The party will claim that a vote for the candidate would throw the election to the opposition party and of course, "We can't let that happen!" Consequently, no matter how good the candidate might be, or how good their ideas, they have virtually no chance of winning.

Whose interests are being served utilizing the tactic? A career politician benefits at the expense of the Nation. A potentially good candidate is defeated merely because his election threatens the political status quo and a self-serving politician's career.

I enjoy reading articles on the political web site PO-LITICO.com. I especially enjoy reading some of the comments readers post. Some of them are insightful, but most only reflect, and serve to perpetuate, the divisiveness that the Democratic Party leadership and Republican Party leadership foist upon us. Through their messaging, the parties' leadership actively promotes the deluding liberal vs. conservative argument, which keeps us divided.

Those leaders understand the power of emotion. They know that by playing on our emotions we can be manipulated. Dr. Elizabeth Ossoff is a psychology professor at Saint Anselm College who specializes in voting behavior. In an article for CNN.com she explained, "voters start from emotion and then get rational." She elaborates by saying, "If you can grab them emotionally, I think you've gone a long way toward getting them where you want them to be, voting either Democrat or Republican." [15]

Anger is an especially powerful emotion. Wikipedia defines anger as "an emotion related to one's psychological interpretation of having been offended, wronged or denied and a tendency to undo that by retaliation." Wikipedia goes on to say, "An angry person may lose his/her objectivity, empathy, prudence or thoughtfulness and may cause harm to others." [16] In other words, when we are angry we are less likely to think rationally or objectively; our natural tendency is to retaliate.

Why is it important for the parties' leadership to keep us divided and angry? Every two years the potential exists for the balance of power to shift in Congress from one party to the other. In 2010 the Republicans wrestled control of the

House from the Democrats. The leadership of the Republican Party assumed the positions of power. The Democratic leadership was relegated to an inferior position. The Republican leadership had been subject to the will of the Democratic leadership during their reign, but now it was their turn. They have the power! They can impose their will on the Democrats!

In 2012 the leadership of the Republican Party wants nothing more than to maintain their hold on power. The leadership of the Democratic Party wants nothing more than for their party to attain the majority so they can be in power again.

Keeping us divided and angry facilitates the leaderships' efforts to attain or maintain the majority so they can maintain their hold on power or to seize power. Their messaging keeps us angry so we won't think rationally and recognize we are being manipulated. Their intent is to keep us focused on retaliation; "We can't let them get away with it anymore!"

Voters

Wake up Indy, please wake up!

In the movie "Indiana Jones and the Temple of Doom," Indiana Jones is forced to drink a foul liquid that puts him in a trance. It effectively turns him into a zombie who is only capable of doing the bidding of his evil masters. As he locks the heroine in a cage, which will be lowered to her certain death in a fiery pit, she pleads, "Wake up Indy, please wake up!" Indiana only comes out of the trance when his sidekick, Shortround, burns him with a torch. Only then does he awaken, save the girl, and save the day.

Voters today are like Indiana Jones in his trance. We are effectively zombies that do the bidding of our political masters. We are asleep to the fact that we are contributing to the slow demise of our Nation by allowing our politicians and the party leaders to pursue their own shortsighted and self-serving interests. Our party masters know they must keep us in a trance to facilitate their pursuit of self-serving and self-aggrandizing interests. If the Nation is sacrificed by their shortsightedness, so be it.

Wake up voters! Please wake up! How many more times must we be burned before we awaken from the trance-inducing effects of "politics as usual" that our political masters foist upon us? They control the two-party system that dominates the entire political process in this country. We must wake up to the reality that our reliance on that system only serves the interests of career politicians and their party leaders.

CHAPTER FOUR

POLITICS, POLITICIANS AND THE GOVERNING PROCESS

In the previous chapter I discussed the influences that affect the patterns of thinking and behaving of stakeholders and how those patterns help to maintain the political status quo for the benefit of career politicians. In this chapter I explain the consequences of our behaviors and their effects on the governing process. Specifically, I focus on politics and politicians.

In our republic (we are not a democracy) we hire, through the elective process, individuals in whom we invest the power and entrust to manage the affairs of our Nation. The Constitution established and legally empowers two groups of representatives to formulate and enact the laws by which we are governed. The two groups are the 100 Senators and the 435 members of the House of Representatives that serve in the Congress of the United States of America.

How often do you hear or use the word politics and politician? They are used so frequently you probably don't even think about their meanings. However, it is important to understand their meanings to understand their effects on how our Nation is governed. Webster's provides several definitions for the word politics. One states that it is, "The methods or tactics involved in managing a government or state." Three definitions are provided for the word politician. They are, "1.a. One actively involved in politics, esp. party politics. b. One who holds or seeks political office. 2. One who seeks personal or partisan gain, often by crafty or dishonest means. 3. One who is skilled or experienced in the science or administration of government."

What does it mean to govern? Again referring to Webster's, it means, "To set forth and administer the public policy and affairs of." What do these definitions mean when put in the context of managing the public policy and affairs of the United States?

When we elect our representatives and send them to Washington we expect them to work collectively to provide long-term solutions for our Nation's problems. We expect them to balance the demands of competing interests and then to reach a consensus on the best courses of action to solve problems. We expect that the politics they engage in, the methods and tactics used to reach their collective decisions, will reflect honest debate and principled deliberation. Certainly not everyone will agree with the outcomes, but if the politics are honest then we have a duty to support those outcomes. This is the governing process we expect. Again, reality is something totally different.

The governing process has been corrupted by political careerism and by the battles for party dominance between the Democratic Party and the Republican Party. The corruption begins even before any election takes place. It starts when candidates affiliate themselves with one of the two parties. They do so because they know that is the only way they can ever be elected. Once they declare that affiliation they are tied to the politics of that party. The party leadership develops the political strategies and messaging their party uses to influence public policy and government administration.

Once they have won their election and get to Washington something happens to them – they turn into politicians. The definition of the word provides clues as to why it happens. They involve themselves in party politics seeking "personal or partisan gain" and achieve their objectives by "crafty or dishonest means." They become skilled in politics, but for what end?

They learn very quickly that the only way they will be able to ascend the seniority ladder and become a party leader is to be a good foot soldier for their party. They learn they must be patient, toe the party line and appease their leadership. Most importantly, they learn they must be elected time and time again. Engaging in politics helps them pursue their self-serving goals.

But, what do we get? Instead of counsels that engage in honest debate and principled deliberation we get counsels whose members make shortsighted decisions based on the need to win the next election. The debate in those counsels falls into the chasm of the partisan divide.

As stated previously, for members of Congress the legislative challenge should be to pursue long-term solutions to our Nation's problems. However, in pursuing long Congressional careers, their focus becomes much more limited in scope and more self-serving in nature. Their real challenge becomes making the correct political decisions – decisions that maximize political gain and/or minimize political risk. Decisions are always made based on the need to win the next election. Savvy career politicians are very successful at the political calculus and get elected time and time again. That allows them to ascend the seniority ladder and to attain the ultimate prize, leadership positions within their respective parties. As leaders they have the power to control the members of their party and perhaps more importantly, the party's message.

Once they have attained positions of leadership within their respective parties, their attention shifts to the partisan political battles in order to be the majority party. They must still win their individual elections, but being incumbents in positions of power makes their seats relatively safe. The ultimate prize for the parties' leadership is to be the leadership of the majority party in Congress.

And why is it so important to be the leadership of the majority party? Power! Congress operates as a pure democracy in which the majority party is in control and has the power. The leadership of the majority party controls the legislative agenda. Also, their party holds the powerful committee chairmanships, which control the execution of the legislative agenda. From their position of power the majority party attempts to impose its will on the minority party and subsequently, on the Nation. Legislative proposals reflect the narrow ideological perspective of the majority party leadership. The minority party leadership and the members of the minority party are relegated to an inferior position and can only respond to the dictates of the majority party and the majority party's legislative proposals. The larger the majority, the greater amount of pressure exerted. Both the majority party and the minority party respond from their narrow ideological perspective. Remember, the party leadership wants to keep us divided and angry. As a result, debate on a proposal devolves into a single argument along the partisan divide. For the majority party leadership, legislative success equates to political advantage, which supports their strategies to maintain the majority. The majority party leadership always wants to maintain their majority so they can retain their hold on power.

The minority party leadership controls their party's response to the majority party's agenda. For them the political calculus revolves around their party's opposition to the majority's actions. Politically they cannot allow the majority party to succeed and must oppose their agenda. Their goal is to garner as much political advantage as they can from their opposition, with the ultimate goal of becoming the majority party. The leadership of the minority party always wants to be the majority party leadership – they want the power! They want to be in control so they can then attempt to impose their will on the other party and subsequently, the Nation.

The leadership of the two parties knows their personal ambitions are tied to the partisan political gain of their parties. Consequently, the politics they engage in has a singular purpose – to improve their party's chances of winning the majority of seats in the next biennial election cycle.

So, how do political careerism and the battles for party dominance corrupt the governing process in this country? Instead of good policies and laws, we get knee jerk reactions to the crisis du jour and shortsighted policy decisions that are intended to pacify voters. As stated previously, long-term solutions are sacrificed on the altar of doing what is politically expedient to win the next election. To enjoy long careers members <u>must</u> make decisions based on the short-term goal of winning the next election. After all, that is what best serves their interests.

Long-term solutions also fall victim to doing what is politically expedient to win the majority. To attain or maintain the majority, party leaders <u>must</u> engage in partisan politics and partisan messaging to maximize the short-term political gain for its members in order to help those members win their elections. After all, that is what best serves their interests.

Since the potential exists for the balance of power to shift every two years, public policy decisions and the administration of the government reflect the imperative requirement to win the most elections in the next biennial cycle. <u>Therefore, governing becomes a mere by-product of the battles for party dominance.</u> In his farewell address Washington warned:

However combinations or associations [parties]...may now and then answer popular ends, they are likely, in the course of time and things, to become potent engines, by which cunning, ambitious, and unprincipled men will be enabled to subvert the power of the people, and to usurp for themselves the reins of government; destroying afterwards the very engines, which have lifted them to unjust domain.

Following are separate commentaries related to the chapter's material.

Fixing America's Politics

On December 14, 2010, POLITCO.com carried a commentary by Robert Reich and Bob Edgar entitled, "Fixing America's politics." Robert Reich served as the Secretary of Labor during the Clinton Administration and Bob Edgar is a former Congressman. Here are a few of their comments:

We love politics. Between us, we've spent more than a half-century in public office and public life. We believe it's important honorable work. So we're deeply distressed at the dysfunctional state of America's political culture. We believe that unless the leaders – in both parties – undertake a comprehensive effort to reform our politics, it will be impossible to make lasting progress to revive our economy, rescue the middle class, corral runaway deficits and solve other national problems.

They acknowledge, "It's hard, frankly, to see how much can be done when so many leaders in both parties seem so intent on destroying the opposition – whatever the cost." Here are two officials that have enjoyed careers in "public office and public life" acknowledging that our political culture contributes to a dysfunctional governing process. I agree wholeheartedly with their assessment! However, I just as wholeheartedly disagree with their source of the solution, the leaders in both parties!

I also find it very interesting that in the article they use the word "games" on two occasions when referring to the political process. In the first instance they are making the reference in the context of campaign cash:

Americans understand that because the game is expensive, candidates and officeholders chase money year-round. That gives benefactors – increasingly large corporations and rich executives – extraordinary power.

In the other instance it is in the context of voter fatigue with the political process:

...too many ordinary citizens – working people, small business owners, students – have simply given up.

They've concluded that the game is rigged against them." [17]

Political careerists think the political process is a game?! For the leadership of the Democratic Party and the Republican Party that is exactly what it is, a game. Winning the game means playing politics better than the opposition party. The party that does the best job playing the game during any given election cycle wins! The ultimate prize is being the majority party in Congress; being the party in power.

Nobody Can Serve Just One

There was once a Lay's potato chip ad that said, "Nobody can eat just one." For our career politicians it's, "Nobody can serve just one." They want to enjoy long careers in "public service" so they can pursue their political ambitions. After all, it seems like a pretty good gig if you can get it. Once they get a "taste" of life in Congress they want to be re-elected again and again and again. Consequently, all the actions they take and all the decisions they make are carefully calculated to enhance their chances of winning the next election.

Breathe It In

Inhale boys and girls. You are now Congressmen and Congresswomen. Breathe deeply your own importance.

After all, you won an election, the party leadership loves you, the media loves you and people want to be seen with you. You're loved and admired...breathe it in.

And, you ain't seen nothin' yet. Just imagine, one day you could be a leader in your party. You might even be Speaker of the House of Representatives. Wow, you could be second in line for the Presidency! Think of how important you will be then. Of course you have to win several more elections and gain the favor of the party leadership to get there. But that's not a problem for you because you know you can be a good foot soldier for your party. You understand that success means biding your time, toeing the party line and appeasing your party's leadership until your day comes. No problem!

But, what about constituents? No sweat. Things are stacked in your favor. Your district was drawn to help you win, you can leverage the power of your incumbency, and, perhaps most importantly, you can leverage the fund raising capacity of your party and amass a large war chest of campaign cash to fend off any challengers.

And, what about those pesky independents voters? Again, no sweat. All you have to do is attack your opponent on some hot button emotional issue and persuade them that you are the lesser-of-the-two-evils.

So go forth and pursue your long careers as politicians. We applaud you. We love you. Thank you for your service. NOT!!!

Tug-of-War

The battles for party dominance can be likened to a tug-of-war. In a tug-of-war teams try to force each other across a line by pulling on a rope. The winner is the team that pulls the other team across the line first.

Today there is a perpetual tug-of-war that rages between Democrats and Republicans to be the majority party in Congress. Congress operates as a pure democracy in which the majority party rules. The "struggle" in this tug-of-war revolves around the immediate necessity of winning as many seats as possible in the next election cycle. After all, the party with the greatest electoral success "wins" the big prize; that party gets to be the majority party – <u>the party in power</u>. Yeaaaaaaa!

However, with a winner comes a loser. Who is the loser in this political tug-of-war for party dominance? Ultimately, we lose. And how do we lose? For party members and their leaders the process of governing is reduced to doing what is politically expedient to pacify voters. Instead of long-term solutions to the Nation's problems we get policies that reflect the short-sighted and short-term necessity of winning as many seats as possible during the next election cycle.

Large Sedan or Compact Car

Ahhhh, don't we just love our two-party system! The Democratic Party and the Republican Party provide such a lovely balance in our country and work so hard for "the

American people." I am so glad that when the ruling party is failing us we can vote and bring the other party to power to rule over us. Then if we become dissatisfied we can return the other party to power. Then if we become dissatisfied we can return the other party to power...and so forth and so on.

It is kind of like being able to choose between only two automobile manufacturers. One sells only large sedans. The other sells only compact cars. Both manufacturers doggedly stick to their business models and promise that their car is the best and the only one the consumer should ever own. They respectively claim, "Big is best!" and "Small is best!"

Where does that leave the consumer? Because the two car manufacturers enjoy a monopoly, consumers must buy either a large sedan or a compact car equipped exactly the way the manufacturer wants. To influence consumers' buying decisions their marketing strategy is primarily based on attacking the other manufacturer's product as inferior and claiming it will not meet consumers' needs.

So, how does the consumer determine which car to buy? Because the choice is limited, the buying decision is reduced to choosing between what the consumer perceives as the better of two bad cars.

Corrupt Debate

In the INTRODUCTION I alluded to this paragraph.

The process of governing has been corrupted because debate on issues revolves around the liberal vs. conservative argument the two parties perpetuate. Either a Democrat or a Republican introduces all legislative proposals. Congressional rules require Independents in Congress to declare if they caucus with the Democrats or conference with the Republicans: in other words, they must choose sides. Because of the liberal vs. conservative argument, half the political spectrum automatically opposes the proposal. Consequently, it is never debated on its merits. Instead debate centers on exploiting the proposal for political gain.

Exempting Themselves

James Madison, who wrote "Federalist No. 10," also authored "Federalist No. 57," which discusses the House of Representatives. Since Senators are also popularly elected (as a result of ratification of the 17th Amendment), the principles also apply to that body and to Congress as a whole. In the paper he discusses the issue of Congress passing laws from which it exempts itself. He puts it in the context of passing oppressive measures:

> ...they [Congress] can make no law which will not have its full operation on themselves and their friends, as well as on the great mass of society. This has always been deemed one of the strongest bonds by which human policy can connect the rulers and the people together. It creates between them that communion of interests and sympathy of sentiments, of which few governments

have furnished examples; but without which every government degenerates into tyranny.

What is to prevent degeneration into tyranny? Madison explains:

If it be asked, what is to restrain [Congress] from making legal discriminations in favor of themselves and a particular class of society? I answer: the genius of the whole system; the nature of just and constitutional laws; and above all, the vigilant and manly spirit which actuates the people of America – a spirit which nourishes freedom, and in return is nourished by it.[18]

He also provides this warning, "If this spirit shall ever be so far debased as to tolerate a law not obligatory on the legislature, as well as the people, the people will be prepared to tolerate any thing but liberty."

In 2010 POLITICO.com carried two reports in which Congress's Office of Compliance stated that Congress had exempted itself from Veteran employment laws and Civil Rights laws.

On July 14th POLITICO reported:

A new report showing that Congress has largely exempted itself from a law that aids post-military employment for vets had lawmakers and veterans groups roiled Wednesday. The report, by the Office of Compliance on the state of the congressional workplace, urges Congress to apply the Veterans Employment Opportunities Act to its own hiring habits. While the law provides veterans with prioritized opportunities to land government jobs, veterans who apply for jobs with the Architect of the Capitol, U.S. Capitol Police, the Congressional Budget Office and some support positions in the House and Senate do not receive this affirmative-action-type boost, potentially preventing veterans from getting jobs.[19]

On July 16th it reported:

Lawmakers from both sides of the aisle took Rand Paul to task when he suggested earlier this year that Title II of the Civil Rights Act of 1964 shouldn't apply to private business. But a new report from Congress's Office of Compliance notes that Congress has never applied the provision to itself.[20]

President Says, "We Deserve Better!"

On August 13, 2011, POLITICO.com carried a report entitled, "Obama: Political system broken." In the report Obama acknowledges that Washington has responded to the country's continuing problems with more "partisanship and gridlock." He says, "So while there's nothing wrong with our country, there is something wrong with our politics, and that's what we have to fix." He acknowledged that we've "got a right to be frustrated" and claims that he is also frustrated. He says we "deserve better." Then he said, "And I don't think it's too much for you to expect that the people you send to this town [Washington, D.C.] start delivering."[21]

Here the President of the United States acknowledges the political process is broken and that we deserve better, the President of the United States! I want to repeat again Charley Reese's comment: "When you fully grasp the plain truth that 545 people exercise complete power over the federal government, then it must follow that what exists is what they want to exist."

Partisanship exists because our elected representatives want it to exist. Whether a Democrat or a Republican, isn't the President a politician? Doesn't he operate within the same broken political system he is berating? Charley Reese also said, "Politicians...are the only people in the world who create problems and then campaign against them." It is a little disingenuous for the President to suggest that Americans should urge their elected officials to put partisanship aside. After all, isn't it well within their purview to do so on their own? Isn't it within Obama's purview to do so himself?

The President, A Partisan Politician

The presidency should be the least partisan of the elected offices in this country. We hire a president to execute the laws of the land, to provide for our security as Commander-in-Chief, and to manage our foreign affairs. However, because he is also deemed the leader of his party, he gets distracted from focusing on the job we hire him to do and instead focuses on the politics of securing his own job and building his party.

We do not pay him to be the partisan focus of his party. Also, we don't pay to support his office so he can engage in partisan political activities. However, because of our entrenched and intransigent two-party system the presidency becomes just another part of the politics we get frustrated about.

If the president truly operated outside the partisan political fray, we might get policy proposals that Congress would look at more objectively rather than through a partisan lens. His motives would be viewed with less suspicion. Also, the perception would be he is more interested in serving the Nation rather than completing the political calculus to secure his re-election. After all, he has a legacy to consider.

But alas, the president's partisan behaviors have become a part of our political culture. As a result his interests and the interests of his party supersede our interests and the imperative need to find long-term solutions to our Nation's problems.

CHAPTER FIVE

WHAT *YOU AND I* MUST DO ABOUT IT PART ONE

In Chapter One I highlighted Albert Einstein's quote on insanity. Another of his quotes is, "We cannot solve our problems with the same thinking we used when we created them." In Chapter Three I explained how we help to maintain the political status quo to our own detriment and the detriment of the Nation by engaging in the "same thinking" that created our corrupt political process. In this chapter I will explain what *you and I* must do to break the cycle of insanity, and to restore our confidence in Congress and integrity to the governing process. *You and I must change our thinking and behaviors.* You and I must propagate a new political culture.

Following the Revolutionary War the Founders knew they needed a new form of government to administer the affairs of the new Nation. In September of 1787 the Constitutional Convention completed its work on the framework for that government, the Constitution of the United States of America.

Benjamin Franklin said the Constitution established the United States of America as a Republic. We refer to our government as a democracy, but it is not. It is a form of democracy, but it is not a democracy in its operation. The Constitution does not even contain the words democracy or democratic. It is very important to understand the distinction between how a republic and a democracy operate.

Webster provides several definitions for the word democracy. The first definition is, "Government exercised either directly by the people or through elected representatives." This definition merely describes what a democracy is. The fourth definition describes how a democracy operates, "Rule by the majority." In a democracy the majority wields power.

Webster also provides several definitions for the word republic. Definition 2.a. states it is, "A political order in which the supreme power is held by a body of citizens who are entitled to vote for officers and representatives responsible to them." This definition provides a description of a republic, but more importantly it specifies that citizens wield power and that their representatives are accountable to them. The actual operation of our republican form of government is framed and given force in the Constitution with its provisions for the Legislative, Executive and Judicial branches, the system of checks and balances, and the mandate for frequent elections.

In Chapter Two I discussed what Madison (Federalist #10) and Washington (Farewell Address) said about the emergence of factions (political parties) in the young Nation. They knew parties would arise. However, they warned factions would have a negative effect on the country and corrupt the governing process. Washington said, "...the common and continual mischiefs of the spirit of party are sufficient to make it the interest and duty of wise people to discourage and restrain it."

Madison stated, "The inference to which we are brought, is, that the causes of faction cannot be removed; and that relief is only to be sought in the means of controlling its effects." He went on to clarify that:

> ...a pure Democracy [one in which the majority rules]... can admit of no cure for the mischiefs of faction. A common passion or interest will, in almost every case be felt by a majority of the whole...there is nothing to check the inducements to sacrifice the weaker party, or an obnoxious individual. Hence it is, that such Democracies have ever been spectacles of turbulence and contention; have ever been found incompatible with personal security, or the rights of property; and have in general been as short in their lives, as they have been violent in their deaths.

Congress operates as a pure democracy. Operating within that framework, the Democratic Party and the Republican Party are incapable of providing a cure for their own political mischief.

Madison explains, "There are two methods of curing the mischiefs of faction: the one, by removing its causes;

the other, by controlling its effects." He explains that removing its causes would destroy liberty, which "is essential to political life." That is not a viable solution.

What was the other solution he recommended? How are we to obtain "relief?" He explains *you and I* must have a plan to "break and control faction."

Among the numerous advantages promised by a well constructed Union, none deserves to be more accurately developed than its tendency to break and control faction. He will not fail therefore to set a due value on any plan which, without violating the principles to which he is attached, provides a proper cure for it.

Madison knew the United States would grow as a country and that growth would also provide the "proper cure":

Extend the sphere, and you take in a greater variety of parties and interests; you make it less probable that a majority of the whole will have a common motive to invade the right of other citizens; or if such motive exists, it will be more difficult for all who feel it to discover their own strength, and to act in unison with each other.

A larger population spread over a greater amount of territory provides for greater and more diverse interests, giving rise to a greater number of parties. When there are more parties it becomes much more difficult for one, or two, to become dominant at the expense of the public good.

We have a misplaced sense of confidence in our two-party system. We really seem to think that the Democratic Party and the Republican Party have all the answers to solve the problems our Nation faces. As long as they maintain their monopoly on power the Nation will never enjoy credible change. To change our political culture, *you and I* must "break and control faction" by rejecting the two parties' tactics to preserve their stranglehold on the political process. *You and I* must explore other political parties and their messaging. As Einstein said, "We cannot solve our problems with the same thinking we used when we created them."

PART TWO

To restore our confidence in Congress and integrity to the governing process in the United States *you and I* must resume our rightful place as the ultimate guardians of that integrity. We must restore republicanism (that is republicanism as in republic and not the party). The remedy we seek is found in George Washington's "Farewell Address to the Nation." He stated:

And, there being constant danger of excess [referring to party excesses], the effort ought to be, by force of public opinion, to mitigate and assuage it. A fire not to be quenched, it demands a uniform vigilance to prevent its bursting into a flame, lest, instead of warming, it should consume.

Washington emphasized that change can only be achieved by the force of public opinion! To rely on our political leaders to affect change is pure folly because it is not in their interests to do so. *You and I* must force change in the system.

First and foremost, we must treat politicians as if they are our employees, because that is exactly what they are. We pay the President $400,000/year and members of Congress $174,000/year (some members make more depending on their position) in financial compensation. We pay their salaries, so that means they work for us. If an employee is not doing his job you can fire him.

We cannot trust the Democratic Party and the Republican Party to provide the needed remedy for the "baneful effects" of their control on the political process in this country. For too long we have placed our trust in the two-party system, which has destroyed the integrity of "public service" and corrupted the governing process. We must no longer allow the shortsighted and self-serving interests of politicians to further erode the long-term health and strength of our Nation. We have done so to our own detriment as their interests have supplanted the interests of constituents and the imperative need to find long-term solutions to the Nation's problems.

Career politicians operating within the two-party system give the impression they are serving "the American people." However, they don't really care about us. If they did they wouldn't behave as if their seats "belonged" to them. That mentality especially applies to Congressional seats where there are no limits on the number of terms a Congressman or Congresswoman can serve. Their behaviors demonstrate that their seats do not belong to us, but rather are only in play each election cycle to see which party will be in the majority.

We must no longer allow them to feel a sense of entitlement that naturally accompanies their being elected time and time again. We must no longer allow them to conduct themselves as though they are unaccountable for their actions, again which naturally occurs when they are elected time and time again. After all, if we keep re-electing them they can justify their behaviors because we validate those behaviors with our votes.

What we need is term limits. Though not specifically written into the Constitution (passage of the 22nd Amendment limited the President to two terms) the Founders knew that frequent rotation in office was important. The Virginia Bill of Rights and the Maryland Bill of Rights, 1780, both had provisions for frequent rotation in office. Article 5 of the Virginia Bill of Rights states:

> That the legislative and executive powers of the state should be separate and distinct from the judiciary; and that the member of the first two may be restrained from oppression, by feeling and participating in the burthens of the people, they should,

at fixed periods, be reduced to a private station, return into that body from which they were originally taken, and the vacancies be supplied by frequent, certain, and regular elections, in which all, or any part of the former members to be again eligible or ineligible, as the laws shall direct.[22]

The Maryland Bill of Rights, 1780, states:

In order to prevent those who are vested with authority from becoming oppressors, the people have a right, at such periods and in such manner as they shall establish by their frame of government, to cause their public officers to return to private life; and to fill up vacant places by certain and regular elections and appointments.[23]

In <u>Federalist No. 57</u>, Madison addressed the House of Representatives. Since Senators are also popularly elected (17th Amendment), the principles also apply to that body. In the paper Madison addressed an issue with the House, stating, "...that it will be taken from that class of citizens which will have least sympathy with the mass of the people, and be most likely to aim at an ambitious sacrifice of the many to the aggrandizement of the few."

Madison recognized exactly what we see today with political careerism: ambitious politicians are aggrandized while we suffer. Recognizing the problem, Madison explained how the Constitution's requirement of frequent elections would provide the solution:

> The aim of every political constitution is, or ought to be, first to obtain for rulers men who possess most wisdom to discern, and most virtue to pursue, the common good of society; and in the next place, to take the most effectual precautions for keeping them virtuous whilst they continue to hold their public trust. The elective mode of obtaining rulers is the characteristic policy of republican government. The means relied on in this form of government for preventing their degeneracy are numerous and various. The most effectual one, is such a limitation of terms of appointments as will maintain a proper responsibility to the people.

The Constitution does not impose term limits on the members of Congress. They were discussed during the Convention, but then rejected because the concept of frequent rotation in office was the accepted norm. Historically, efforts to legislatively impose them have failed. The Supreme Court declared States' efforts to impose term limits on their Congressional representatives unconstitutional. Congress has failed to act on its own proposals to impose terms limits on its members. After all, it works counter to their interests to do so.

The term limits I am referring to would be voluntary. Candidates would serve in accordance with the Founding tradition of the citizen legislator – one who serves for limited periods of time and then returns to private life to be subject to the laws they helped pass. George Washington, who could have been king of the United States, or at least President for life, set the example by only serving two terms.

You and I must find and elect candidates whose definition of "public service" really is about, and genuinely involves, the public. These are candidates whose interests to serve their constituents and the Nation supersede the desire for self-aggrandizement and power. These are candidates that recognize the corrupting influences of our political system and how our political culture facilitates that corruption. *You and I* must elect citizen legislators who will shun the allure of political careerism and its corrupting influences. In <u>Federalist No.57</u> Madison provided the following guidance:

> Who are to be the objects of popular choice? Every citizen whose merit may recommend him to the esteem and confidence of his country. No qualification of wealth, of birth, of religious faith, or of civil profession is permitted to fetter the judgment or disappoint the inclination of the people.

In declaring the Nation's independence from England, Thomas Jefferson stated the Nation was going to provide "new Guards for their [its] future Security." It is time *you and I* find New Guards, citizen legislators, to provide for our future security. It has taken well over 100 years for our po-litical culture to become anchored by the Democrats' and Republicans' battles for party dominance. It will take time to unravel the complexity of that culture. However, as we find and elect ever-increasing numbers of New Guards, our future will indeed be more secure. Over time, the allure of political careerism will fade and the process of governing will no longer fall victim to the all-encompassing necessity of winning that next election.

CHAPTER SIX

IN CONCLUSION

In the Forward I explained that our political process is suffering from an illness – a type of insanity. Throughout the book I provided evidence about how our political culture helps to maintain the political status quo and how, in spite of our frustration and low opinion of Congress, our patterns of thinking and behaving actually contribute to our own frustration and low opinion of Congress. I explained how maintaining the political status quo benefits career politicians to our detriment and the detriment of the Nation.

In Chapter One, I exclaimed, "America, we have a problem!" I talked about how NASA engineers took materials available to the astronauts of Apollo 13 and built a contraption to reduce the buildup of carbon dioxide in the capsule. The astronauts had the means to build the same contraption, but more importantly, they had the motivation and will to do so. Again, there were no guarantees of success, but if the astronauts had not followed the engineers' instructions, they would have surely died.

Much like the carbon dioxide in the capsule of Apollo 13, our Nation's political process is toxic. Just as the NASA engineers and the astronauts on Apollo 13 did, we must take what is available to us, the process of frequent elections, to resume our rightful place of power in the political process. But, do we have the motivation? Do we have the will? Do we value the political status quo so much that we will deny ourselves the opportunity to change our thinking and, consequently, our behaviors? Do we want to continue having such a low opinion of Congress? Do we want to continue to experience the dysfunctional nature of our political process? Do we want to continue to watch politicians behave in ways that are self-serving and self-aggrandizing? Do we want to continue being second-class citizens in the political process?

Again, the cure for our illness is found in the Constitution – frequent elections. However, we must change the way we think about elections and change our behaviors as voters. We must use elections to restore integrity to the governing process and to restore our confidence in Congress. We must use elections to resume our rightful place as the ultimate power in our republic. We must use elections to force accountability by causing frequent rotation in office. We must use elections to break the stranglehold the Democratic Party and the Republican Party have on the political process.

Armed with the knowledge contained in this book we can change our political culture and no longer be unwitting accomplices in helping career politicians pursue their self-serving interests.   Remember, as Washington said, it is only "by force of public opinion" that credible change will take place.

You and I can make it happen! You and I must make it happen!

CHAPTER SEVEN

THE DECLARATION OF INDEPENDENTS

The Declaration of Independents was the first document I wrote during my self-study of our country's political process. It was also the first document I published on the web. I wrote it to explain why we need to break our ties with the two major political parties.

Since publishing it, I have learned that a modification to the Declaration of Independence, entitled the "Declaration of Sentiments – Seneca Falls," was used during a convention on women's rights held at Seneca Falls, New York, in 1848. Elizabeth Cady Stanton and Lucretia Mott authored the modification.

The Seneca Falls convention is recognized as the initiating event of the women's rights and suffrage movement in the United States, which eventually led to the passage of the 19th Amendment to the Constitution giving women the right to vote. Their efforts led to a significant change in the Nation's political culture. So, in the effort to promote change in our current political culture, I feel I am in good company.

The Declaration of Independents

Please note: italicized words are taken from the original Declaration of Independence.

When in the course of our Nation's events *it becomes necessary* for We the People of the United States to dissolve the *bands which have connected us* with the major political parties and to again assume the powers granted us by the Constitution, *a decent respect to the opinions of mankind requires that* we *should declare the causes which impel* us *to the separation.*

We hold these truths to be self evident, that all men are created equal, that they are endowed by their Creator with certain unalienable Rights, that among these are Life, Liberty and the pursuit of Happiness. That to secure these rights, Governments are instituted among Men, deriving their just powers from the consent of the governed. That whenever political parties *become destructive to these ends, it is the Right of the People to alter or abolish* that party system *and to institute a new* system *laying its foundation on such principles and organizing its powers in such form as to them shall seem most likely to affect their Safety and Happiness. Prudence, indeed, will dictate that* political parties *so long established should not be abandoned for light and transient causes; and accordingly all experience hath shown that* We the People *are more disposed to suffer, while evils are sufferable, than to right* ourselves by breaking the ties that bind us to the major parties. *But when a long train of abuses and usurpations* by the major parties actually work to the detriment of We the People it is our right; indeed it is our duty to throw off such parties *and to provide new guards for* our *future security. Such has been the patient sufferance* of We the People of the United States *and such is now the necessity which constrains* us to change the status quo and requires us to sever ties with the major political parties. The history of the major parties is a history of repeated injuries and usurpations all having the direct object of nullifying government "of the people, by the people, for the people" and replacing it with government of the parties, by the parties and for the parties. To prove this, the following facts are submitted:

The major parties evolved and maintain their existence in spite of the Founding Father's warnings of the evils of powerful political parties.

The major parties have a monopoly on the entire political process in the United States.

The major parties are more interested in obtaining and maintaining power, especially at the federal level, than they are in effective governance.

The major parties erect barriers to competition to protect their monopoly by controlling the means to be elected, including the money, media and machinery (organization).

Unless a candidate for elective office is a member of one of the major parties there is little chance the candidate will be elected. This has created a defacto unconstitutional qualification for elective office.

Citizens are effectively disenfranchised in presidential elections because the major parties effectively dictate the candidates for President and Vice President.

Partisanship is the norm with each party brandishing a "Whip" to ensure conformance to the party line on important votes.

Fundamental differences between the parties have narrowed in spite of ideological claims to the contrary. The only exception is during presidential elections when the candidates appeal to the "base" of their parties during the primaries.

The majority party controls the implementation of the rules in the House and Senate, effectively controlling which legislation reaches the "floor" of each respective chamber for a vote.

The major parties have consolidated power at the federal levels in direct violation of the Constitution of the United States.

These examples of abuse and usurpation demonstrate how the major parties monopolize the political process at our expense. We the People of the United States have been rendered virtually impotent in the process of governance. Recognizing the results of the usurpation and abuses of the major parties, We the People of the United States *solemnly publish and declare* that we are free and independent voters and that our ties to the major parties are absolved and that we no longer owe allegiance to the major parties or their perceived ideologies.

Notes

1. Newport, Frank. <u>Congress' Job Approval at New Low of 10%: Republicans and Democrats equally negative.</u> Gallup.com. Retrieved from http://www.gallup.com/poll/152528/Congress-Job-Approval-New-Low.aspx
2. CNN. "Super Tuesday forces delay of stimulus vote." CNN.com, January 31, 2008. Retrieved from http://articles.cnn.com/2008-01-31/politics/economy.stimulus_1_stimulus-package-extension-of-unemployment-insurance-aides?_s=PM:POLITICS
3. Reese, Charley. "545 people are responsible for the mess, but they unite in a common con." Orlando Sentinel, July 30, 2011.com. Retrieved from http://articles.orlandosentinel.com/2011-07-30/news/os-ed-charley-reese-545-people-1984-073111_1_tax-code-president-vetoes-con-game
4. Hellriegel, Don and John W. Slocum, Jr. (2010). <u>Organizational Behavior</u>. 2011 Custom Edition. Cengage Learning. Mason, Ohio
5. The Library of Congress/Thomas. <u>The Federalist Papers</u>. Retrieved from http://thomas.loc.gov/home/histdox/fedpapers.html

6. Yale Law School/The Avalon Project. Washington's Farewell Address – 1796. Retrieved from http://avalon.law.yale.edu/18th_century/washing.asp

7. Beck, Glenn. An Inconvenient Book. 2007. Threshold Editions. New York, New York.

8. Wikipedia. "Sophism." Wikipedia.org. Retrived from http://en.wikipedia.org/wiki/Sophistry

9. Superville, Darlene. "Obama says GOP must back US first, create jobs." Associated Press. Retrieved from http://news.yahoo.com/obama-says-gop-must-back-us-first-create-182721246.html

10. Burns, Alexander. "Dems push back with torrent of polls." POLITICO.com. Retrieved from http://dyn.politico.com/printstory.cfm?uuid=4139438B-B5C1-C951-1E836ECE40489E11

11. Burns, Alexander. "Polls become another spin weapon." POLITICO.com. Retrieved from http://dyn.politico.com/printstory.cfm?uuid=7F092F62-F7D6-2A49-0A8ACF3D8B7FD1F1

12. Bastiat, Frederic. The Law. 1993. The Foundation for Economic Education, Inc. Hudson-On-Hudson, New York.

13. Ellul, Jacques. Propaganda: The Formation of Men's' Attitudes. February 1973. Vintage Books, New York.

14. Hartman, Rachel Rose. "Poll suggests 2012 change in power in Washington." Yahoo.com, Ticket Blog. August 12, 2011. Retrieved from http://news.yahoo.com/blogs/ticket/poll-suggests-2012-change-power-washington-131541841.html

15. Keck, Kristi. "Angry voters could affect both parties." CNN.com. January 25, 2010. Retrieved from http://articles.cnn.com/2010-01-25/politics/voter. anger_1_democrat-martha-coakley-republicans-midterm?_s=PM:POLITICS

16. Wikipedia. "Anger." Wikipedia.org. Retrived from http://en.wikipedia.org/wiki/Anger

17. Edgar, Bob and Robert Reich. "Fixing America's Politics." POLITICO.com. Retrieved from http://dyn.politico.com/printstory. cfm?uuid=E2F763B2-07CC-6CD5-64FFB841E34697EB

18. Constitution.org. "The Federalist No. 57." Retrieved from http://www.consitution.org/fed/federa57.html

19. Cogan, Marin and Erika Lovley. "Hill exempts self from veterans' law." POLITICO.com. Retrieved from http://dyn.politico.com/printstory. cfm?uuid=CE871ECF-18FE-70B2-A80D25884C-F1ADE2

20. Lovely, Erika. "Congress exempt from Civil Rights Act." POLITICO.com. Retrieved from http://dyn.politico.com/printstory.cfm?uuid= D8CEA102-18FE-70B2-A89A2341B85C0901

21. Phillip, Abby. "Obama, Political system broken." POLITICO.com. Retrieved from http://dyn.politico.com/printstory.cfm?uuid= 2150C346-283D-4137-A86D-A515C767696D

22. Constitution.org. "The Virginia Declaration of Rights." June 12, 1776. Retrieved from http://www.constitution.org/bor/vir_bor.htm

23. National Humanities Institute.org. "A Declaration of the Rights of the Inhabitants of the Commonwealth of Massachusetts." 1780. Retrieved from http://www.nhinet.org/ccs/docs/ma-1780.htm